Bond

Verbal Reasoning

10 Minute Tests

9–10 years

Frances Down

OXFORD
UNIVERSITY PRESS

Underline the two words in each line which are most similar in type or meaning.

Example   <u>dear</u>   pleasant   poor   extravagant   <u>expensive</u>

1	flexible	rigid	stiff	friendly	clever
2	table	mirror	basin	door	bath
3	apple	pear	carrot	rose	nettle
4	busy	clear	stormy	quick	obvious
5	lorry	aeroplane	boat	yacht	train

Underline the two words, one from each group, which are the most opposite in meaning.

Example   (dawn, <u>early</u>, wake)   (<u>late</u>, stop, sunrise)

6	(tidy, burn, flame)	(neat, messy, fire)
7	(house, soft, concrete)	(hard, cement, stable)
8	(right, river, solid)	(liquid, rigid, water)
9	(confident, timid, bashful)	(careful, tearful, shy)
10	(high, over, beside)	(through, under, above)

Underline the pair of words most similar in meaning.

Example   come, go   <u>roam, wander</u>   fear, fare

11	half, crumb	complete, whole	right, wrong
12	grip, clasp	release, hold	balance, fall
13	answer, question	repair, spoil	problem, difficulty
14	appear, arrive	come, go	disappear, return
15	warm, cool	climb, drop	feel, touch

Underline the word in brackets that is most opposite in meaning to the word in capitals.

Example   WIDE   (broad   vague   long   <u>narrow</u>   motorway)

16	GIVE	(present	grant	result	spare	take)
17	FLAT	(house	even	odd	bumpy	high)
18	BELOW	(under	above	on	beneath	between)
19	SHINY	(dull	quick	cloud	metal	sum)
20	END	(corner	side	beginning	middle	top)

Total [   ]

Underline the one word in the brackets which will go equally well with both the pairs of words outside the brackets.

Example   rush, attack   cost, fee   (price, hasten, strike, <u>charge</u>, money)

1   leave, separate   piece, share   (bit, portion, part, holiday, section)

2   beat, punch   success, achievement   (hit, smack, purpose, thump, give)

3   box, case   stem, torso   (tree, trunk, luggage, suitcase, body)

4   shiny, glowing   clever, intelligent   (dull, light, bright, smart, quick)

5   dig, sow   tree, bush   (leaf, vegetable, spade, rake, plant)

Underline the two words which are the odd ones out in the following groups of words.

Example   black   <u>king</u>   purple   green   <u>house</u>

6   shirt   vest   socks   shoes   trousers

7   ferry   bicycle   yacht   skateboard   windsurfer

8   eyes   hat   nose   mouth   glove

9   middle   edge   bottom   border   side

10   safe   secure   sausage   sound   sick

Rearrange the muddled letters in capitals to make a proper word. The answer will complete the sentence sensibly.

Example   A BEZAR is an animal with stripes.   _ZEBRA_

11   Two TNNIOCNTES of the world are Africa and Asia.   _____

12   The storm brought down an ECLETRCI cable.   _____

13   Don't forget to lock the RTOFN door!   _____

14   We are going to the ASEDIES on Saturday if it is sunny.   _____

15   Sarah loves ice cream with COHCOTELA sauce.   _____

Find and underline the two words which need to change places for the sentence to make sense.

Example   She went to <u>letter</u> the <u>write</u>.

16   Dairy give us cows products.

17   Number other is on the twenty side of the street.

18   Some were given you homework.

19   Can you close door the please?

20   My red is blue and shirt.

Total

Add one letter to the word in capital letters to make a new word. The meaning of the new word is given in the clue.

Example PLAN   simple   ___plain___

1 HAIR   seat   _____
2 SPED   pay out   _____
3 ROOF   evidence   _____
4 SALLOW   not deep   _____
5 HEEL   car part   _____

Find a word that is similar in meaning to the word in capital letters and that rhymes with the second word.

Example CABLE   tyre   ___wire___

6 FOOTWEAR   two   _____
7 MASTER   sword   _____
8 NARRATE   smell   _____
9 MOULDY   mail   _____
10 SHATTER   take   _____

Underline the two words that are made from the same letters.

Example TAP   PET   <u>TEA</u>   POT   <u>EAT</u>

11	DANCE	LANCE	LANES	CRANE	CLEAN
12	SLOPE	POLES	POSTS	LEAPS	PEEPS
13	FLAIR	FIRES	RIFLE	FRAIL	ROOFS
14	SWIRL	LOWER	WINGS	SWING	GRINS
15	LEAST	LASTS	STOOL	SLIPS	TALES

Rearrange the letters in capitals to make another word. The new word has something to do with the first two words.

Example spot   soil   SAINT   ___STAIN___

16 chair   bench   TEAS   _____
17 bound   jump   PALE   _____
18 cord   string   PORE   _____
19 fall   drip   PROD   _____
20 instruct   train   CHEAT   _____

4

Total

Selecting Words

Underline two words, one from each group, that go together to form a new word. The word in the first group always comes first.

Example (hand, <u>green</u>, for) (light, <u>house</u>, sure)

1 (hand, foot, way) (signal, path, shoe)
2 (green, apple, wood) (picker, leaf, land)
3 (straw, hay, pink) (berry, cloud, stick)
4 (old, bald, handy) (horse, tyre, man)
5 (white, blue, clean) (bath, wash, sky)

Find the letter which will end the first word and start the second word.

Example peac (h) ome

6 pla (____) ard 7 thin (____) ing
8 blu (____) yes 9 fou (____) eal
10 flo (____) ind

Complete the following sentences by selecting the most sensible word from each group of words given in the brackets. Underline the word selected.

Example The (<u>children</u>, boxes, foxes) carried) the (houses, <u>books</u>, steps) home from the (greengrocer, <u>library</u>).

11 Michael picked up the (oars, rubbish, pigeon) and expertly (climbed, talked, rowed) the boat to the (castle, shore, school).
12 The (rocket, train, promise) blasted into the (sky, rails, room) from the space (station, town, letter).
13 Mrs Patel (dropped, carried, drove) her car (under, into, between) the parking space and (sped, cleaned, turned) off the engine.
14 My (uncle, aunt, dog) Trevor is my (pet's, mother's, desk's) (chair, brother, wall).
15 Mr Bowen bent (up, down, along) to smell the (fragrant, cold, easy) rose in his (garden, bathroom, cupboard).

Underline the one word which **cannot be made** from the letters of the word in capital letters.

Example	STATIONERY	stone	tyres	ration	<u>nation</u>	noisy
16	RAINSTORM	stain	month	train	mains	roast
17	FAVOURABLE	blare	flour	brave	flavour	bluff
18	MARGARINE	argue	grain	margin	grime	enigma
19	HINDQUARTERS	quart	trend	strand	quince	trade
20	CRISPBREAD	price	pears	brisk	drape	pride

5

Total

Test 5: **Finding Words**

Find the four-letter word hidden at the end of one word and the beginning of the next word. The order of the letters may not be changed.

Example   The children had bat<u>s and</u> balls.   <u>sand</u>

1   Please wait for me.   _____

2   Your football team is good this season.   _____

3   Jane painted her room peach and cream.   _____

4   I need to remember to lock the front door.   _____

5   Please stick the label to your jacket.   _____

Find the three-letter word which can be added to the letters in capitals to make a new word. The new word will complete the sentence sensibly.

Example   The cat sprang onto the MO.   <u>USE</u>

6   She has grown her H long.   _____

7   We went to France for our HOLI.   _____

8   The village shop S at six o'clock yesterday.   _____

9   The ambulance RUD the sick person to hospital.   _____

10   Every morning Luke eats a B of cereal.   _____

Find a word that can be put in front of each of the following words to make new, compound words.

Example   cast   fall   ward   pour   <u>down</u>

11   berry   board   currant   bird   _____

12   cuff   bag   rail   shake   _____

13   pot   spoon   cake   time   _____

14   stairs   stream   standing   roar   _____

15   boat   buoy   span   less   _____

Move one letter from the first word and add it to the second word to make two new words.

Example   hunt   sip   <u>hut</u>   <u>snip</u>

16   fair   way   _____   _____

17   march   cob   _____   _____

18   every   early   _____   _____

19   teach   flee   _____   _____

20   climb   path   _____   _____

Total

TEST 6: Alphabetical Order and Substitution

Underline the word in each line that has its letters in alphabetical order.

1	flare	flour	floor	fable	feeds
2	hosts	hilly	hello	hares	hinge
3	apply	above	acorn	adept	after
4	badger	better	believe	begging	begins
5	dwell	dizzy	defrost	deity	dense

If these words were written backwards and then placed in alphabetical order, which word would come fifth? Underline your answer.

6	ladle	paddle	little	stile	female
7	garland	garage	gallant	galaxy	gadget
8	goodness	fairness	kindness	sadness	likeness
9	biscuit	racket	ticket	chariot	bucket
10	nears	bears	fears	rears	tears

If A = 13, B = 10, C = 8, D = 6 and E = 1, find the answers to the following calculations.

11 A – E = _____

12 BD = _____

13 (B – C) + D = _____

14 C + D + E = _____

15 (A – C) + D = _____

If A = 2, B = 3, C = 5, D = 6 and E = 10, give the answer to each of these calculations as a letter.

16 E – C = _____

17 B + A + C = _____

18 D ÷ A = _____

19 E – (B + C) = _____

20 A × B = _____

7

Total

Look at the first group of three words. The word in the middle has been made from the other two words. Complete the second group of three words in the same way, making a new word in the middle.

Example   PA<u>IN</u>   IN<u>TO</u>   <u>TO</u>OK   ALSO   <u>SOON</u>   ONLY

1	FEES	SINK	INKY	POST	_____	REEK
2	DEAR	ARCH	CHIP	MOST	_____	ARMY
3	BOAT	OATS	PINS	PEAS	_____	GOAT
4	GEAR	GOLF	WOLF	CROW	_____	SLAM
5	PART	PANE	WINE	EXAM	_____	KNIT

Change the first word into the last word, by changing one letter at a time and making a new, different word in the middle.

Example   CASE   <u>CASH</u>   LASH

6	BIRD	_____	WIND
7	TASK	_____	WALK
8	BELT	_____	BALL
9	WING	_____	SONG
10	FAME	_____	FARM

Change the first word of the third pair in the same way as the other pairs to give a new word.

Example   bind, hind   bare, hare   but, <u>hut</u>

11	take, teak	mate, meat	sale, _____
12	list, silt	last, salt	left, _____
13	fate, rate	fake, rake	fail, _____
14	wind, find	wool, fool	wall, _____
15	tops, spot	leer, reel	keep, _____

Find the missing number by using the two numbers outside the brackets in the same way as the other sets of numbers.

Example   2 [8] 4   3 [18] 6   5 [25] 5

16	7 [15] 8	6 [9] 3	13 [__] 3
17	2 [1] 2	4 [2] 2	6 [__] 3
18	4 [8] 2	4 [12] 3	3 [__] 5
19	13 [2] 11	21 [9] 12	16 [__] 8
20	3 [9] 3	8 [16] 2	5 [__] 4

Total

TEST 8: Logic

Read the statements and then underline two of the five options below that must be true.

1–2 'Some roofs are made of tiles. All houses have roofs.'

All roofs are made of tiles.   All houses have tiles.
Tiles are a type of roof covering.   Straw can be a roof covering.
A house needs a roof.

3–4 'The police help to keep us safe and catch criminals. Some police officers wear helmets.'

Police officers must wear helmets at all times.   Police officers often work in pairs.
Helmets may be part of a police officer's uniform.   People feel safer when there is less crime.
Police officers help to catch people who break the law.

In a pet shop there are 5 hutches in a row. A different rabbit is in each hutch. Work out, from the clues, where each rabbit belongs.

1	2	3	4	5

The black rabbit is next to the white rabbit with red eyes.
The floppy eared rabbit is in one of the end hutches.
The fat rabbit is not next to the brown and white rabbit, and it is further to the right than the floppy eared rabbit.
The brown and white rabbit is between the floppy eared rabbit and the white rabbit.

5–9 HUTCH 1 _____   HUTCH 3 _____   HUTCH 5 _____

HUTCH 2 _____   HUTCH 4 _____

Sam and Otis play football.   Bob, Mike and Ravi play football and cricket.
Tom, Mike and Sam play rugby.   Everyone likes computer games except Ravi.

10   Who likes cricket and rugby?   _____

11   How many children like computer games?   _____

12   Who likes rugby but not football?   _____

13   How many children like football but not computer games?   _____

14   Who likes football and rugby but not cricket?   _____

Janet's bookshelves are divided into 6 areas. She keeps different items in each section. From the information below, work out what goes into each section.

A	B
C	D
E	F

The novels are directly above the reference books.
The novels are directly to the right of the CDs.
The photographs are directly to the left of the DVDs.
The DVDs are above the novels.
The CDs are higher than the school books but lower than the photos.

15–20   novels ____   reference books ____   CDs ____

school books ____   photographs ____   DVDs ____

9

Time for a break! Go to Puzzle Page 42 ▶

Total

TEST 9: **Codes**

Test time: 0 · · · · 5 · · · · 10 minute

Here are the number codes for four words. Match the right code to the right word.

BEND	BIND	BOOK	KIND
6538	0138	6138	6440

1 BEND _____

2 BIND _____

3 BOOK _____

4 KIND _____

5 Using the same code, decode 8435. _____

Solve the problems by working out the codes.

6 If 7914 is the code for FOUR, what does 794 stand for? _____

7 If 5612 is the code for MACE, what does 1652 stand for? _____

8 If 9461 is the code for PORE, what does 6491 stand for? _____

9 If 4813 is the code for CART, what does 183 stand for? _____

10 If 6972 is the code for TAME, what does 726 stand for? _____

Solve the problems by working out the letter codes. The alphabet has been written out to help you.

A B C D E F G H I J K L M N O P Q R S T U V W X Y Z

Example In a code, SECOND is written as UGEQPF.
How would you write THIRD? ___VJKTF___

11 In a code, BISCUIT is written as CJTDVJU. How would you write BITS? _____

12 In a code, STEAM is written as UVGCO. How would you write MAST? _____

13 In a code, BRING is written as CSJOH. How would you write BEEN? _____

14 In a code, WHITE is written as VGHSD. How would you write HEEL? _____

15 In a code, PRIME is written as NPGKC. How would you write FOUL? _____

16 In a code, DREAM is written as GUHDP. Decode PDGH. _____

17 In a code, BRAIN is written as FVEMR. Decode RIIH. _____

18 In a code, GRIME is written as FQHLD. Decode FDQL. _____

19 In a code, FLOUR is written as DJMSP. Decode BCCN. _____

20 In a code, DRESS is written as CQDRR. Decode AHSD. _____

10

Total _____

Choose two words, one from each set of brackets, to complete the sentence
in the best way.

Example   Smile is to happiness as (drink, <u>tear</u>, shout) is to (whisper, laugh, <u>sorrow</u>).

1   River is to water as (stream, vein, fridge) is to (cold, blood, kitchen).

2   Winter is to cold as (summer, spring, fire) is to (log, hot, sunshine).

Complete the following sentence in the best way by choosing one word from
each set of brackets.

Example   Tall is to (tree, <u>short</u>, colour) as narrow is to (thin, white, <u>wide</u>).

3   Fish is to (fingers, pond, gills) as man is to (car, lungs, dinner).

4   Begin is to (finish, start, continue) as end is to (rear, finish, bottom).

5   Pause is to (break, snap, claws) as halt is to (go, start, stop).

Fill in the missing letters and numbers. The alphabet has been written out to help you.

A B C D E F G H I J K L M N O P Q R S T U V W X Y Z

Example   AB is to CD as PQ is to <u>RS</u>.

6   ZX is to YW as XV is to ____.

7   Ae is to Fj as Ko is to ____.

8   ST is to UV as WX is to ____.

9   P3 is to O5 as N7 is to ____.

10   HJ is to JL as LN is to ____.

Give the missing numbers and letters in the following sequences.

Example   2   4   6   8   10   <u>12</u>

11	24	20	16	12	8	____
12	6	7	9	____	16	21
13	5	____	13	17	21	25
14	101	202	____	404	505	606
15	15t	17t	19u	21u	____	25v

Give the missing letters in the following sequences.
The alphabet has been written out to help you.

A B C D E F G H I J K L M N O P Q R S T U V W X Y Z

Example   CQ   DP   EQ   FP   GQ   <u>HP</u>

16	EK	GL	____	KN	MO	OP
17	MN	____	OR	PT	QV	RX
18	PQ	PR	____	QT	RU	RV
19	PZ	QX	PV	QT	PR	____
20	Gu	____	Is	Jr	Kq	Lp

Total [   ]

TEST 11: **Mixed**

Test time: 0 .... 5 .... 10 minute

Rearrange the muddled letters in capitals to make a proper word. The answer will complete the sentence sensibly.

Example   A BEZAR is an animal with stripes.   ZEBRA

1   If I make mistakes with my pencil, I use my BURREB.   _____

2   At the beach I play with my TECKUB and spade.   _____

3   In AUJANYR the weather is likely to be cold.   _____

4   A bee or wasp GNIST is painful.   _____

5   If you light matches near petrol there will be an ELXOPSOIN. _____

6   At RITCHSMAS we sing carols.   _____

Answer these questions. The alphabet has been written out to help you.

A B C D E F G H I J K L M N O P Q R S T U V W X Y Z

7   Put the letters in the word SPECIAL in alphabetical order.   _____

8   Which is now the fifth letter?   _____

9   Put the letters in the word PREACH in alphabetical order.   _____

10   Which is now the fourth letter?   _____

Find a word that is similar in meaning to the word in capital letters and that rhymes with the second word.

Example   CABLE   tyre   wire

11   MARK   mane   _____   **12**   TERROR   deer   _____

13   SHOP   moor   _____   **14**   PRESERVE   wave   _____

15   WICKED   while   _____

Solve the problems by working out the codes.

16   If the code for FLAMES is SDQRPN, what is the code for SEAM?   _____

17   If the code for BLAST is XNRFE, what is the code for STALL?   _____

18   If the code for QUITE is 59432, what is the code for TIE?   _____

19   If the code for TWIST is bxyzb, what is the code for SIT?   _____

20   If the code for SLUMP is FTRXY, what is the code for PLUM?   _____

If these words were listed in reverse alphabetical order, which word would come second?

1	brooch	break	bracken	bruise	bridge	_____
2	chimney	choose	cherub	cheek	chapel	_____
3	penguin	pedal	penny	peony	pecan	_____
4	darkness	danger	dancing	dampen	dainty	_____

Solve the problems by working out the codes.

5   If 8641 is the code for TEAS, what does 1648 stand for?   _____

6   If 3996 is the code for GOOD, what does 693 stand for?   _____

7   If 6752 is the code for MITE, what does 5762 stand for?   _____

8   If 8491 stands for GRAB, what does 194 stand for?   _____

Complete the following expressions by filling in the missing word.

Example   Pen is to ink as brush is to ____*paint*____.

9   Kennel is to dog as stable is to _____.

10   Cushion is to chair as pillow is to _____.

11   Butterfly is to six legs as bird is to _____ legs.

12   Picture is to wall as rug is to _____.

Town A is directly north of Town B.
Town C is west of B but south of D.
If the towns make a square on a map, where is

13   D in relation to A?   _____   **14**   A in relation to C?   _____

15   D in relation to B?   _____   **16**   B in relation to D?   _____

If A = 24, B = 12, C = 8, D = 4 and E = 2, give the answer to these calculations as a letter.

17 $A \div B =$ _____   **18** $B + C + D =$ _____

19 $(B - C) + D =$ _____   **20** $\dfrac{DE}{E} =$ _____

Total

TEST 13: Mixed

Find the three-letter word which can be added to the letters in capitals to make a new word. The new word will complete the sentence sensibly.

Example The cat sprang onto the MO. ___USE___

1 The queen does not often wear a CN. _____

2 Nadia laid the table with four knives and KS. _____

3 That grocery S is more expensive than the one we use. _____

4 WE you knocked your head, you have a bruise. _____

5 The PR went out so we sat by candlelight all night. _____

Which one letter can be added to the front of all these words to make new words?

Example _C_ are   _C_ at   _C_ rate   _C_ all

6 ____ ass   ____ ink   ____ ray   ____ at

7 ____ how   ____ at   ____ even   ____ and

8 ____ our   ____ oal   ____ ox   ____ ear

9 ____ pen   ____ range   ____ at   ____ men

Fill in the missing letters and numbers. The alphabet has been written out to help you.

A B C D E F G H I J K L M N O P Q R S T U V W X Y Z

Example AB is to CD as PQ is to RS.

10 GH is to KL as OP is to ____.

11 DF is to HJ as LN is to ____.

12 M8 is to L9 as K10 is to ____.

13 Mn is to Qr as Uv is to ____.

14 ZX is to VT as RP is to ____.

15 ST is to QR as OP is to ____.

Underline the word in the brackets closest in meaning to the word in capitals.

Example UNHAPPY (unkind   death   laughter   sad   friendly)

16 TRAIL   (measure   ward   pass   home   path)

17 HONOUR   (obey   lord   praise   order   hot)

18 PETROL   (oil   car   garage   engine   fuel)

19 DISCOVER   (hide   treasure misplace find   purchase)

20 CRIMSON   (blue   red   paint   flower   sky)

14

Total

Test time: 0 ⌇⌇⌇⌇⌇⌇⌇⌇⌇⌇⌇ 5 10 minutes

Underline the two words, one from each group, which are closest in meaning.

Example (race, shop, start) (finish, begin, end)

1 (conceal, jelly, carnival) (show, mask, mould)
2 (danger, past, menace) (threaten, safety, annoy)
3 (orange, skin, huge) (body, colour, peel)
4 (tape, tune, melon) (melody, worm, violin)
5 (excited, happy, miserable) (smile, cry, sad)

Here are some symbol codes for four words. Match the right codes to the right words.

BOOT	BROW	TRAY	WARY
? Q + =	X 5 5 ?	£ + Q =	X Q 5 £

6 BOOT _____
7 BROW _____
8 TRAY _____
9 WARY _____

Using the same code, decode:

10 £ + Q ? _____
11 Q 5 5 ? _____

Give the missing numbers and letters in the following sequences.

Example 5 21 8 17 11 13 14 9

12	4	___	6	6	8	9	10	12
13	Q8	B5	Q10	B6	Q12	B7	___	B8
14	a17	a4	___	b5	c13	c6	d11	d7
15	42	F	35	H	___	J	21	L
16	3	5	6	___	9	9	12	11

If P = 2, Q = 3, R = 4, S = 14 and T = 15, find the answer to the following calculations.

17 $\frac{S}{P} + Q =$ _____

18 $S - QR =$ _____

19 $\frac{T}{Q} + R =$ _____

20 $S + PQ =$ _____

15

Total _____

Add one letter to the word in capital letters to make a new word.
The meaning of the new word is given in the clue.

Example   PLAN   simple   ___plain___

1   FEED   released   _____

2   FIST   before second   _____

3   LENT   sloped   _____

4   EAVES   departs   _____

Solve the problems by working out the letter codes. The alphabet has been written out to help you.

A B C D E F G H I J K L M N O P Q R S T U V W X Y Z

Example   In a code, SECOND is written as UGEQPF.
How would you write THIRD? ___VJKTF___

5   In a code, READY is written as SFBEZ. What is YARD?   _____

6   In a code, BARKS is written as DCTMU. What is WIND?   _____

7   In a code, TOKEN is written as RMICL. What is SOCK?   _____

8   In a code, CRESS is written as BQDRR. What is BEST?   _____

9   In a code, HOUSE is written as FMSQC. What is SHOE?   _____

10   In a code, FARMS is written as HCTOU. What is FAIL?   _____

Change the first word of the third pair in the same way as the other pairs to give a new word.

Example   bind, hind   bare, hare   but, ___hut___

11   bore, robe   dome, mode   file, _____

12   rail, bail   rush, bush   rook, _____

13   fare, fear   lane, lean   lake, _____

14   town, down   tusk, dusk   trip, _____

15   tale, late   lose, sole   newt, _____

16   doom, mood   draw, ward   flow, _____

If $A = 15$, $B = 12$, $C = 8$, $D = 3$ and $E = 1$, find the answer to the following calculations.

17 $A - C =$ _____

18 $(B + C) - E =$ _____

19 $\dfrac{A}{D} =$ _____

20 $(B - C) + D =$ _____

Total

Test time: 0 |||||||||| 5 |||||||||| 10 minutes

Underline the one word which **cannot be made** from the letters of the word in capital letters.

Example   STATIONERY   stone   tyres   ration   <u>nation</u>   noisy

1	GABERDINE	greed	engine	bread	drain	bride
2	DASTARDLY	tardy	yards	saddle	darts	astral
3	APOLOGISE	goals	spool	pages	igloo	police
4	NEWSPAPER	wasps	spear	prawns	spare	preen
5	APPARATUS	strap	sprat	parts	arrest	traps

Find the four-letter word hidden at the end of one word and the beginning of the next word. The order of the letters may not be changed.

Example   The children had bat<u>s and</u> balls.   _____sand_____

6	Mum buys fruit at the market.	_____
7	That is my best arrangement today.	_____
8	I will brush my teeth another time.	_____
9	Half the class wandered in late.	_____
10	Must I brush under the desks too?	_____

Move one letter from the first word and add it to the second word to make two new words.

Example   hunt   sip   _____hut_____   _____snip_____

11	play	sap	_____	_____
12	loft	lock	_____	_____
13	quite	have	_____	_____
14	stool	fits	_____	_____

Give the missing letters and numbers in the following sequences.
The alphabet has been written out to help you.

A B C D E F G H I J K L M N O P Q R S T U V W X Y Z

Example   CQ   DP   EQ   FP   GQ   <u>HP</u>

15	CF	CG	DH	DI	____	EK
16	____	vE	wF	xG	yH	zI
17	DW	EV	FU	____	HS	IR
18	AB	____	CF	DH	EJ	FL
19	OP	RQ	ST	VU	WX	____
20	W13	Y11	____	Y7	W5	Y3

17

Time for a break! Go to Puzzle Page 43 ▶

Total _____

Fill in the crosswords so that all the given words are included.
You have been given one letter as a clue in each crossword.

1–3

SHARD   STIFF

FIXED   SNOWS

INDIA

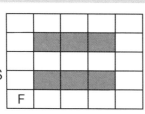

4–6

DARES   ANGER

BRAIN   BEARD

NOTES

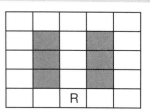

Underline the two words which are the odd ones out in the following groups of words.

Example   black   <u>king</u>   purple   green   <u>house</u>

7	hockey	cricket	ball	players	rounders
8	mouse	gerbil	rat	shark	cobra
9	oak	rose	sunflower	willow	tulip
10	book	television	newspaper	radio	magazine

Find the letter which will complete both pairs of words, ending the first word and starting the second. The same letter must be used for both pairs of words.

Example   mea (t) able   fi (t) ub

11	pin (____) ing	tal (____) ey
12	sta (____) elp	sill (____) es
13	pal (____) xam	to (____) agle
14	gri (____) ie	gras (____) ig

Here are some symbol codes for four words. Match the right code to the right word.

FADE	FIND	DEAN	NEED
! / @ %	@ £ £ %	! * % £	% £ * @

15	FADE	_____	16	FIND	_____
17	DEAN	_____	18	NEED	_____

Using the same code, decode:

19	% / @ £ _____	20	% £ * ! _____

Total

Test time: 0 | | | | | 5 | | | | | 10 minutes

Underline the one word in the brackets which will go equally well with both the pairs of words outside the brackets.

Example   rush, attack   cost, fee   (price, hasten, strike, <u>charge</u>, money)

1	fete, festival	even, just	(party, level, proper, fair, equal)
2	foolhardy, reckless	spots, redness	(rush, rash, acne, fever, silly)
3	build, construct	force, cause	(order, make, stack, assemble, form)
4	difficult, tough	firm, inflexible	(easy, solid, hard, complicated, strong)
5	copy, mimic	shadow, trail	(follow, model, stalk, obey, lead)

The drama club is putting on a school play. Tessa and Harriet are going to make the costumes. Nadeen and Ben are going to build the sets. Francesca is going to help with the costumes but also do the lights. Mick is going to be the announcer for the first half of the play and Tessa will be the announcer for the second half. Mick will also be in charge of moving the props on and off the stage. Ben will help Mick when he is busy as the announcer.

6   Which two students are doing only one job?   _____ and _____

7   Which student is helping with the costumes and the lights?   _____

8   How many students are helping make the costumes?   _____

9   Who will help move the props during the first half of the play?   _____

10   Which two students won't be busy during the play? _____ and _____

Find the letter which will end the first word and start the second word.

Example   peac (h) ome

11   foo (____) humb   **12**   nex (____) rain   **13**   sta (____) elt   **14**   fee (____) ost

Rearrange the muddled letters in capitals to make a proper word. The answer will complete the sentence sensibly.

Example   A BEZAR is an animal with stripes.   _ZEBRA_

15   Under the stairs there is a dark BOADRPUC.   _____

16   The moon was shining so BRGTYIHL, it lit up the room.   _____

17   Vijay's father parked the car in the GGREAA.   _____

18   Sixteen, seventeen, IHENEEGT, nineteen.   _____

19   A young goose is called a LNGGISO.   _____

20   My mother enjoys doing crossword ZSZLEPU.   _____

19

Total

Underline the two words in each line which are most similar in type or meaning.

Example   <u>dear</u>   pleasant   poor   extravagant   <u>expensive</u>

1   steer   drive   garden   pond   swift
2   wed   flower   marry   church   feast
3   son   neighbour   daughter   friend   student
4   hair   heart   arm   neck   leg
5   school   scheme   letter   film   plan

Change the first word into the last word, by changing one letter at a time and making a new, different word in the middle.

Example   CASE   ___CASH___   LASH

6   CUBE   _____   TUNE
7   PALM   _____   CALF
8   PINE   _____   PICK
9   WARM   _____   YARN

Fill in the missing letters and numbers. The alphabet has been written out to help you.

A B C D E F G H I J K L M N O P Q R S T U V W X Y Z

Example   AB is to CD as PQ is to R̲S̲.

10   JK is to LM as NO is to ____.
11   S16 is to T14 as U12 is to ____.
12   3FG is to 5GH as HI7 is to ____.
13   De is to Fg as Vw is to ____.
14   TR is to SQ as RP is to ____.
15   AD is to EH as IL is to ____.

Look at the first group of three words. The word in the middle has been made from the other two words. Complete the second group of three words in the same way, making a new word in the middle.

Example   PAI<u>N</u>   INTO   <u>T</u>OOK   ALSO   ___SOON___   ONLY

16   PEEL   LOVE   OVEN   BOSS   _____   HUTS
17   INTO   TORE   REAP   MOTH   _____   INCH
18   SHUN   HUNT   WILT   SPAT   _____   FISH
19   STAR   SOLD   HOLD   MOOR   _____   LICE
20   KIND   KING   RUNG   ZERO   _____   NEST

(20)

Total [   ]

Test 20: Mixed

Underline the two words which are the odd ones out in the following groups of words.

Example   black   <u>king</u>   purple   green   <u>house</u>

1	knife	fork	bowl	plate	spoon
2	stable	cow	elephant	sheep	sty
3	desk	ruler	class	rubber	pencil
4	spring	rain	winter	snow	summer
5	Australia	Wales	London	Sweden	Paris

Look at the first group of three words. The word in the middle has been made from the other two words. Complete the second group of three words in the same way, making a new word in the middle.

Example   PAIN   INTO   TOOK   ALSO   <u>SOON</u>   ONLY

6	PAST	STUN	UNTO	WIFE	_____	ARCH
7	RAKE	RUST	MUST	STAR	_____	BEAT
8	DRAG	DRIP	SNIP	FALL	_____	SUNG
9	SPAR	PART	WENT	TREE	_____	HOOF
10	SLUG	GONE	ONES	SLIM	_____	AREA

Add one letter to the word in capital letters to make a new word.
The meaning of the new word is given in the clue.

Example   PLAN   simple   <u>plain</u>

11	RIGHT	shiny	_____	**12**	BUSH	broom	_____
13	TONE	rock	_____	**14**	FAME	fire	_____

15–20   Here are two rows of houses in a street. Work out which families live in each house.

22	24	26
ARMADA AVENUE		
21	23	25

The Bennetts and the Ashtons live directly next door to each other on the even side of the street.
The Bennetts live in a lower number than the Ashtons.
The Fish family live directly opposite the Catt family.
The Bennetts live directly opposite to the Smiths who live in a higher number than the Catts, next door.
The Jones family are best friends with the Fish family.

Bennett _____   Ashton _____   Fish _____

Catt _____   Smith _____   Jones _____

Total [   ]

Test time: 0 .... 5 .... 10 minutes

Give the missing numbers and letters in the following sequences.

Example 2   4   6   8   10   _12_

1	14	24	___	44	54	64
2	3	___	11	15	19	23
3	___	10	15	20	25	30
4	4	5	7	10	___	19
5	X13	Y11	Z9	___	Y5	Z3
6	64	32	16	8	4	___

Solve the problems by working out the codes.

7 If the code for x o – + is DOWN, what does the code + o x stand for? _____

8 If the code for < > / \ is SANG, what does the code \ > < stand for? _____

9 If the code for APPQ is DOOR, what does the code QPA stand for? _____

10 If the code for = – ~ \ is THIS, what does the code \ ~ = stand for? _____

Rearrange the letters in capitals to make another word. The new word has something to do with the first two words.

Example spot   soil   SAINT   _STAIN_

11	loved	adored	READ	_____
12	light	fire	PARKS	_____
13	painful	hurting	ROSE	_____
14	killed	dead	NAILS	_____
15	frozen	water	DICE	_____
16	ruler	guide	DEALER	_____

Find a word that can be put in front of each of the following words to make new compound words.

Example cast   fall   ward   pour   _down_

17	side	vent	to	sure	_____
18	knob	mat	step	bell	_____
19	times	where	thing	one	_____
20	world	wear	water	stand	_____

22

Total

Test time: 0 | | | | | 5 | | | | | 10 minutes

Find the three-letter word which can be added to the letters in capitals to make a new word. The new word will complete the sentence sensibly.

Example   The cat sprang onto the MO.   ___USE___

1   I hope we win some G medals at the Olympics.   _____
2   My grandmother wears a HING aid.   _____
3   Have a bowl of STBERRIES and cream.   _____
4   Would you like jam and TER on your bread?   _____
5   During the lunch H Tom plays football.   _____

Underline the one word which **can be made** from the letters of the word in capital letters.

Example   CHAMPION   camping   notch   peach   cramp   <u>chimp</u>

6	KINDEST	stink	desks	token	taste	kings
7	ELEPHANT	thank	neater	paler	panel	heaps
8	PARTITION	nation	print	parting	north	trains
9	CONTAINER	energy	conker	narrow	counter	ration
10	BRIGHTLY	height	truly	light	tight	highly

Remove one letter from the word in capital letters to leave a new word. The meaning of the new word is given in the clue.

Example   AUNT   an insect   ___ANT___

11	DRIVE	plunge	_____
12	GRIND	smile	_____
13	BLAST	final	_____
14	TRANCE	copy	_____

Give the missing letters and numbers in the following sequences. The alphabet has been written out to help you.

ABCDEFGHIJKLMNOPQRSTUVWXYZ

Example   CQ   DP   EQ   FP   GQ   <u>HP</u>

15	Z12	Y10	X8	W6	V4	___
16	___	GW	HV	IU	JT	KS
17	MZ	MY	___	NW	OV	OU
18	kV	IU	mT	___	oR	pQ
19	Ny	___	Pw	Qv	Ru	St
20	AB	DC	EF	HG	___	LK

23

Total

Underline two words, one from each group, that go together to form a new word. The word in the first group always comes first.

Example   (hand, <u>green</u>, for)   (light, <u>house</u>, sure)

1	(hand, foot, close)	(sore, writing, reading)
2	(dripping, wet, towel)	(suit, clothes, tea)
3	(price, much, too)	(more, kind, less)
4	(car, engine, wheel)	(boot, near, barrow)

Give the missing numbers and letters in the following sequences.

Example   5   21   8   17   11   13   <u>14</u>   9

5	3	10	5	11	7	12	___	13
6	___	r	9	s	12	t	15	u
7	R15	R1	___	S2	T17	T3	U18	U4
8	A7	1a	B7	2b	C7	3c	D7	___
9	1	2	3	5	5	___	7	11

Underline the pair of words most similar in meaning.

Example   come, go   <u>roam, wander</u>   ear, fare

10	whisper, shout	discuss, talk	argue, agree
11	block, lump	chunk, morsel	part, whole
12	up, down	outside, exterior	under, on
13	high, low	loud, faint	quiet, hushed
14	find, keep	enter, exit	fall, tumble

Change the first word of the third pair in the same way as the other pairs to give a new word.

Example   bind, hind   bare, hare   but, _____hut_____

15	wane, wean	pale, peal	bare, _____
16	top, lop	tight, light	tax, _____
17	pals, slap	deer, reed	draw, _____
18	made, dame	file, life	lope, _____
19	mean, mane	weak, wake	team, _____
20	chin, thin	chat, that	chose, _____

24

Total

Answers

TEST 1: SIMILARS AND OPPOSITES

1 rigid, stiff
2 basin, bath
3 apple, pear
4 clear, obvious
5 boat, yacht
6 tidy, messy
7 soft, hard
8 solid, liquid
9 confident, shy
10 over, under
11 complete, whole
12 grip, clasp
13 problem, difficulty
14 appear, arrive
15 feel, touch
16 take
17 bumpy
18 above
19 dull
20 beginning

TEST 2: SORTING WORDS 1

1 part
2 hit
3 trunk
4 bright
5 plant
6 socks, shoes
7 bicycle, skateboard
8 hat, glove
9 middle, bottom
10 sausage, sick
11 CONTINENTS
12 ELECTRIC
13 FRONT
14 SEASIDE
15 CHOCOLATE
16 dairy, cows
17 other, twenty
18 some, you
19 door, the
20 red, shirt

TEST 3: SORTING WORDS 2

1 CHAIR
2 SPEND
3 PROOF
4 SHALLOW
5 WHEEL
6 shoe
7 lord
8 tell
9 stale
10 break
11 LANCE CLEAN
12 SLOPE POLES
13 FLAIR FRAIL
14 WINGS SWING
15 LEAST TALES
16 SEAT
17 LEAP
18 ROPE
19 DROP
20 TEACH

TEST 4: SELECTING WORDS

1 footpath
2 woodland
3 strawberry
4 handyman
5 whitewash
6 y

7 k
8 e
9 r
10 w
11 oars rowed shore
12 rocket sky station
13 drove into turned
14 uncle mother's brother
15 down fragrant garden
16 month
17 bluff
18 argue
19 quince
20 brisk

TEST 5: FINDING WORDS

1 form
2 hiss
3 hand
4 tore
5 belt
6 AIR
7 DAY
8 HUT
9 SHE
10 OWL
11 black
12 hand
13 tea
14 up
15 life
16 fir away
17 arch comb
18 ever yearly
19 each fleet
20 limb patch

TEST 6: ALPHABETICAL ORDER AND SUBSTITUTION

1 floor
2 hilly
3 adept
4 begins
5 dirty
6 little
7 galaxy
8 fairness
9 chariot
10 tears
11 12
12 60
13 8
14 15
15 11
16 C
17 E
18 B
19 A
20 D

TEST 7: WORD PROGRESSIONS

1 TREE
2 STAR
3 EAST
4 CLAM
5 EXIT
6 BIND
7 TALK
8 BELL
9 SING
10 FARE
11 seal
12 felt
13 rail
14 fall
15 peek
16 16
17 2
18 15
19 8
20 20

TEST 8: LOGIC

1–2 Tiles are a type of roof covering.
A house needs a roof.

3–4 Helmets may be part of a police officer's uniform. Police officers help to catch people who break the law.

5–9
1 floppy eared
2 brown and white
3 white
4 black
5 fat

10 Mike
11 5
12 Tom
13 1
14 Sam

15–20 novels D
reference books F
CDs C
school books E
photographs A
DVDs B

TEST 9: CODES

1 6538
2 6138
3 6440
4 0138
5 DONE
6 FOR
7 CAME
8 ROPE
9 RAT
10 MET
11 CJUT
12 OCUV
13 CFFO
14 GDDK
15 DMSJ
16 MADE
17 NEED
18 GERM
19 DEEP
20 BITE

TEST 10: SEQUENCES

1 vein, blood
2 summer, hot
3 gills, lungs
4 start, finish
5 break, stop
6 WU
7 Pt
8 YZ
9 M9
10 NP
11 4
12 12
13 9
14 303
15 23v
16 IM
17 NP
18 QS
19 QP
20 Ht

TEST 11: MIXED

1 RUBBER
2 BUCKET
3 JANUARY
4 STING
5 EXPLOSION
6 CHRISTMAS
7 ACEILPS
8 L
9 ACEHPR
10 H
11 stain
12 fear
13 store
14 save
15 vile
16 NPQR
17 FERNN
18 342
19 zyb
20 YTRX

Bond 10 Minute Tests: Verbal Reasoning 9–10 years

TEST 12: MIXED

1 brooch	10 bed
2 chimney	11 two
3 penny	12 floor
4 danger	13 west
5 SEAT	14 north-east
6 DOG	15 north-west
7 TIME	16 south-east
8 BAR	17 E 19 C
9 horse	18 A 20 D

TEST 13: MIXED

1 ROW	8 f	15 MN
2 FOR	9 o	16 path
3 HOP	10 ST	17 praise
4 HER	11 PR	18 fuel
5 OWE	12 J11	19 find
6 p	13 Yz	20 red
7 s	14 NL	

TEST 14: MIXED

1 conceal, mask	10 WART
2 menace, threaten	11 ROOT
3 skin, peel	12 3
4 tune, melody	13 Q14
5 miserable, sad	14 b15
6 X 5 5 ?	15 28
7 X Q 5 £	16 7
8 ? Q + =	17 10
9 £ + Q =	18 2
	19 9
	20 20

TEST 15: MIXED

1 FREED	8 ADRS	15 went
2 FIRST	9 QFMC	16 wolf
3 LEANT	10 HCKN	17 7
4 LEAVES	11 life	18 19
5 ZBSE	12 book	19 5
6 YKPF	13 leak	20 7
7 QMAI	14 drip	

TEST 16: MIXED

1 engine	5 arrest
2 saddle	6 them
3 police	7 star
4 wasps	8 than

9 swan	14 tool, fists
10 shun	15 EJ 18 BD
11 pay, slap	16 uD 19 ZY
12 lot, flock	17 GT 20 W9
13 quit, heave	

TEST 17: MIXED

1–3

S	N	O	W	S
T				H
I	N	D	I	A
F				R
F	I	X	E	D

4–6

B	R	A	I	N
E		N		O
A		G		T
R		E		E
D	A	R	E	S

7 ball, players	9 oak, willow
8 shark, cobra	10 television, radio
	11 k
	12 y
	13 e
	14 p
	15 ! * % £
	16 ! / @ %
	17 % £ * @
	18 @ £ £ %
	19 DINE
	20 DEAF

TEST 18: MIXED

1 fair	10 Harriet and Nadeen
2 rash	11 t 13 b
3 make	12 t 14 l
4 hard	15 CUPBOARD
5 follow	16 BRIGHTLY
6 Harriet and Nadeen	17 GARAGE
7 Francesca	18 EIGHTEEN
8 3	19 GOSLING
9 Ben	20 PUZZLES

TEST 19: MIXED

1 steer, drive	11 V10
2 wed, marry	12 IJ9
3 son, daughter	13 Xy
4 arm, leg	14 QO
5 scheme, plan	15 MP
6 TUBE	16 SHUT
7 CALM	17 THIN
8 PINK	18 PATH
9 WARN	19 MICE
10 PQ	20 ZEST

TEST 20: MIXED

1 bowl, plate	3 desk, class
2 stable, sty	4 rain, snow

5 London, Paris	11 BRIGHT
6 FEAR	12 BRUSH
7 SEAT	13 STONE
8 FANG	14 FLAME
9 REEF	15 24 18 21
10 MARE	16 26 19 23
	17 22 20 25

TEST 21: MIXED

1 34	8 GAS	15 ICED
2 7	9 ROD	16 LEADER
3 5	10 SIT	17 in
4 14	11 DEAR	18 door
5 X7	12 SPARK	19 some
6 2	13 SORE	20 under
7 NOD	14 SLAIN	

TEST 22: MIXED

1 OLD	8 print	15 U2
2 EAR	9 ration	16 FX
3 RAW	10 light	17 NX
4 BUT	11 DIVE	18 nS
5 OUR	12 GRIN	19 Ox
6 stink	13 LAST	20 IJ
7 panel	14 TRACE	

TEST 23: MIXED

1 handwriting	12 outside, exterior
2 wetsuit	13 quiet, hushed
3 priceless	14 fall, tumble
4 wheelbarrow	15 bear
5 9	16 lax
6 6	17 ward
7 S16	18 pole
8 4d	19 tame
9 8	20 those
10 discuss, talk	
11 block, lump	

TEST 24: MIXED

1 8F9	9 them
2 13	10 shoot, fire
3 17	11 train, teach
4 15H	12 pair, two
5 love	13 diary, journal
6 item	14 road, street
7 sour	15 MBOE
8 thin	16 LHMS

17 PCKN 19 CBMM
18 CDRJ 20 EPGB

Test 25: Mixed

1	kind, cruel	12	15e
2	more, less	13	20
3	clean, dirty	14	9
4	answer, question	15	A3
5	begin, turn	16	PARTS STRAP
6	at, were	17	LEAPT PLATE
7	channels, television	18	SPOOL LOOPS
8	hose, garden	19	DEALER LEADER
9	burnt, spread	20	STEAL LEAST
10	swing, sister		
11	25		

Test 26: Mixed

1	PLAY	8	correct	16	JI
2	EATS	9	frequent	17	RS
3	FOOL	10	mature	18	NL
4	ONCE	11	t	19	9TU
5	SNOW	12	h	20	W55
6	fast	13	s		
7	straight-forward	14	l		
		15	EG		

Test 27: Mixed

1	relaxed, strict	10	exciting, book, chapter
2	soft, firm	11	5
3	wealthy, poor	12	6
4	stale, fresh	13	1
5	elephants, river, trunks	14	40
6	road, right, traffic	15	WEED
7	ran, ball, goal	16	FIRM
8	playground, put on, coats	17	HURT
9	pencil, over, bin	18	FOUR
		19	LIFE
		20	BIRD

Test 28: Mixed

1	PEACH CHEAP	3	TRACE CRATE
2	TOAST STOAT	4	ASLEEP PLEASE

5 STATE TASTE 12 Ann
6 beef, cow 13 Beth
7 radio, listen 14 Chloe
8 black, grey 15 3
9 dawn, dusk 16 LOMN
10 apple, fruit 17 TRA
11 bedroom, sleep 18 SBYF
  19 AZC
  20 WZTL

Test 29: Mixed

1	b	5	first	9	JADE
2	l	6	accent	10	ICED
3	s	7	blot	11	6145
4	h	8	hilly	12	8554

13–14 Cars travel on roads. Roads are for vehicles to travel on.

15–16 My cat is related to a lion. The cat family includes tigers.

17 6 18 11 19 22 20 12

Test 30: Mixed

1	is, at	11	1836
2	road, bus	12	6481
3	for, had	13	3814
4	go, please	14	1446
5	trees, leaves	15	SEAT
6	in, put	16	dearest
7	wholesome	17	beast
8	upset	18	please
9	indeed	19	yearn
10	windscreen	20	eager

Test 31: Mixed

1–3

P	L	A	N	K
	E		O	
W	A	R	T	S
	V		E	
S	E	N	D	S

4–6

B	R	A	N	D
A				R
R	A	N	G	E
B				A
S	H	R	E	D

7 905
8 @ $! %
9 UQB
10 × − = +
11 marmalade
12 tiger
13 collar
14 C B
15 D B
16 A D
17 whole, part
18 delicate, hardy
19 believe, doubt
20 anxious, carefree

Test 32: Mixed

1	LEAP	8	sun	15	6
2	LEMON	9	child	16	424
3	QUIET	10	foot	17	12
4	SLEET	11	N	18	D42
5	DIAL	12	M	19	3
6	CHARM	13	N	20	17
7	post	14	L		

Test 33: Mixed

1	PJ	12	iced
2	IR	13	then
3	E5	14	team
4	DP	15	leaf
5	GH	16	stench, smell
6	SB	17	join, connect
7	b	18	bend, curve
8	a	19	pen, pencil
9	g	20	need, require
10	t		
11	harm		

Test 34: Mixed

1	WENT	10–15	card F plastics G brown glass B shoes E green glass C newspapers A
2	DRAB		
3	FAME		
4	EACH		
5	FLAT		
6	bedrooms		
7	ink	16	sketch
8	a nose	17	fowl
9	long ears	18	quick
		19	light
		20	rule

Test 35: Mixed

1–3

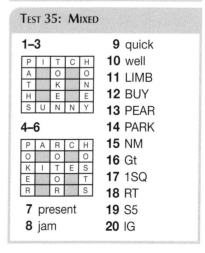

P	I	T	C	H
A		O		O
T		K		N
H		E		E
S	U	N	N	Y

4–6

P	A	R	C	H
O		O		O
K	I	T	E	S
E		O		T
R		R		S

7 present
8 jam
9 quick
10 well
11 LIMB
12 BUY
13 PEAR
14 PARK
15 NM
16 Gt
17 1SQ
18 RT
19 S5
20 IG

Test 36: Mixed

1	S11	11	WILL
2	14	12	POLE
3	9	13	POST
4	40	14	LOOP
5	X9	15	FILE
6	8	16	alive
7	1	17	expensive
8	10	18	release
9	2	19	sluggish
10	CRAB	20	patterned

Test 37: Mixed

1 5793
2 1379
3 9375
4 1375
5 BREAD
6 hooves, paws
7 cricket, hockey
8 difficult, easy
9 loose, tight
10 hurl, toss
11 entrance, arrival

12–15 *Give one mark for each two correct answers:* Spain A, shirt C, yellow B, orange B, hat C, van D, Norway A, bus D

16 mend
17 tender
18 value
19 hollow
20 ignorant

Test 38: Mixed

1 higher
2 stork
3 paths
4 front
5 torch
6 mauls
7 skate
8 throne
9 braid
10 snare
11 fan, seal
12 ear, brainy
13 sore, bend
14 heat, thorn
15 GN
16 Z11
17 Gr
18 JK
19 VI
20 SL

Test 39: Mixed

1 bizarre, weird
2 prize, value
3 near, by
4 precious, valuable
5 tatters, shreds
6 DATE
7 BOAT
8 CART
9 PAIN
10 E
11 B
12 B
13 E

14–15 The Atlantic is one of the world's oceans.
There are oceans in the world.

16 WIG
17 WIT
18 KEEP
19 ATOM
20 LOT

Test 40: Mixed

1 HIDE
2 FEED
3 4935
4 31754
5 4516
6 plate, knife
7 thunder, lightning
8 seagulls, sheep
9 newsagent, newspapers
10 car, man
11 red, green
12 15
13 collie
14 10
15 dalmatian
16 pet, baby
17 slow, kind
18 remove, carry
19 frame, crayon
20 rude, scowling

Puzzle ❶

Puzzle ❷

CAMP
ROUND **FIRE**
WATER **WORK** PLACE
WHEEL SHOP **OUT** MAT
CHAIR FRONT SIDE **DOOR** TIN
TABLE WAYS **MAN** STOP
CLOTH **AGE** KIND
LESS HEARTED
ON

TURN
OVER NIP
HAND GROWN PER
SOME FULL UP FORM
HOW TIME LOAD ALL LESS
EVER SHARE RIGHT ROUND
GREEN HOLDER WING
HOUSE MIRROR
WIFE

Puzzle ❸

ROUTE C

	HO	ME	↑	↑					
	SWEET	HOME	←	←	←	↑			
						↑			
						↑			
					←	←	↑		
							↑		
							↑		
				↑	→	→			

Puzzle ❹

Any 5 words that can be made from each of the listed words, for example:

FLOWER
row   wore   lower
for   owe   wolf   owl
GARDEN
den   dare   anger
red   darn   range
SPRING
pig   grin   sprig
rig   ring   grins   pin
LEAVES
veal   leave   ale
seal   slave   see

Puzzle ❺

Children	Colour of Dice	Number of Sixes
Mia	red	12
Nathan	yellow	7
Rohan	blue	14
Sita	green	5

TEST 24: Mixed

Give the missing numbers and letters in the following sequences.

Example   2   4   6   8   10   _12_

1	3A4	4B5	5C6	6D7	7E8	____
2	9	____	17	21	25	29
3	13	15	____	19	21	23
4	____	20H	25G	30G	35F	40F

Find the four-letter word hidden at the end of one word and the beginning of the next word. The order of the letters may not be changed.

Example   The children had bat<u>s and</u> balls.   ____sand____

5   The policeman's helmet fell over his eyes.   _____

6   She gave me my favourite magazine.   _____

7   We will miss our turn.   _____

8   The twins are both in the show.   _____

9   "Best foot forwards!" shouted the major.   _____

Underline the two words, one from each group, which are closest in meaning.

Example   (race, shop, <u>start</u>)   (finish, <u>begin</u>, end)

10   (wood, camp, shoot)   (tent, metal, fire)

11   (bus, train, chair)   (school, sit, teach)

12   (pair, many, plenty)   (single, two, none)

13   (note, diary, poem)   (drawing, map, journal)

14   (path, road, pavement)   (park, street, city)

Solve the problems by working out the letter codes. The alphabet has been written out to help you.

A B C D E F G H I J K L M N O P Q R S T U V W X Y Z

Example   In a code, SECOND is written as UGEQPF.
How would you write THIRD?   ____VJKTF____

15   In a code, LAYER is written as MBZFS. What is LAND?   _____

16   In a code, SLEEP is written as RKDDO. What is MINT?   _____

17   In a code, PLAIN is written as RNCKP. What is NAIL?   _____

18   In a code, GUESS is written as FTDRR. What is DESK?   _____

19   In a code, THROW is written as UISPX. What is BALL?   _____

20   In a code, FUDGE is written as DSBEC. What is GRID?   _____

Time for a break! Go to Puzzle Page 44 ▶

TEST 25: **Mixed**

Underline the two words, one from each group, which are most opposite in meaning.

Example (dawn, <u>early</u>, wake)   (<u>late</u>, stop, sunrise)

1 (nurse, divide, kind)   (sort, cruel, caring)

2 (most, more, least)   (less, lose, some)

3 (clean, misty, clear)   (dirty, spotless, shiny)

4 (speak, talk, answer)   (question, reply, whisper)

Find and underline the two words which need to change places for the sentence to make sense.

Example   She went to <u>letter</u> the <u>write</u>.

5 Begin over your papers and turn.

6 There at over thirty children were the party.

7 The channels will not change television.

8 He watered the hose with a garden.

9 Edith burnt butter on her spread toast.

10 Sometimes I push my little swing on the sister.

Give the missing numbers and letters in the following sequences.

Example   5   21   8   17   11   13   <u>14</u>   9

11	6	30	7	___	8	20	9	15
12	11e	20y	13e	15y	___	10y	17e	5y
13	C	14	E	17	G	___	I	23
14	10	12	8	___	6	6	4	3
15	A9	X5	A7	X5	A5	X5	___	X5

Underline the two words which are made from the same letters.

Example   TAP   PET   <u>TEA</u>   POT   <u>EAT</u>

16	PARTS	STARE	STRAP	RESTS	PRESS
17	STEEL	LEAST	TAUPE	LEAPT	PLATE
18	PROUD	SPOOL	LOOPS	DROOP	SOUPS
19	DEALER	READER	TREADS	LEADER	SPREAD
20	STEAL	LEAST	STOOL	LASTS	STALL

Total [   ]

Look at the first group of three words. The word in the middle has been made from the other two words. Complete the second group of three words in the same way, making a new word in the middle.

Example   PAIN   INTO   TOOK   ALSO   ___SOON___   ONLY

1	KIND	DROP	ROPE	DEEP	_____	LAYS
2	DRAG	RAGE	FINE	NEAT	_____	CATS
3	WANT	WIRE	FIRE	FOOT	_____	TOOL
4	LATE	TEST	STOW	MOON	_____	CENT
5	PINE	PEAT	WHAT	STUN	_____	FLOW

Underline one word in the brackets which is most opposite in meaning to the word in capitals.

Example   WIDE   (broad   vague   long   <u>narrow</u>   motorway)

6	SLOW	(loose	fast	last	sluggish	late)
7	TRICKY	(awkward	clever	difficult	straightforward	sly)
8	WRONG	(correct	faulty	mistaken	untrue	unsure)
9	RARE	(unusual	front	back	smooth	frequent)
10	IMMATURE	(unripe	childish	young	mature	long)

Which one letter can be added to the front of all these words to make new words?

Example   _c_ are   _c_ at   _c_ rate   _c_ all

11	____ each	____ ouch	____ ear	____ high
12	____ our	____ ill	____ earth	____ air
13	____ mile	____ tuck	____ pill	____ pin
14	____ ice	____ edge	____ earn	____ ate

Fill in the missing letters and numbers. The alphabet has been written out to help you.

A B C D E F G H I J K L M N O P Q R S T U V W X Y Z

Example   AB is to CD as PQ is to RS.

15   BD is to CE as DF is to ____.
16   PO is to NM as LK is to ____.
17   Lm is to No as Pq is to ____.
18   QO is to PN as OM is to ____.
19   15QR is to 13RS as 11ST is to ____.
20   T22 is to U33 as V44 is to ____.

Total

Underline the pair of words most opposite in meaning.

Example cup, mug coffee, milk <u>hot, cold</u>

1	relaxed, strict	stone, rock	garden, house
2	pillow, bed	cushion, chair	soft, firm
3	luxury, riches	wealthy, poor	money, coins
4	stale, fresh	calm, peaceful	magical, fantastic

Complete the following sentences by selecting the most sensible word from each group of words given in the brackets. Underline the words selected.

Example The (<u>children,</u> books, foxes) carried the (houses, <u>books,</u> steps) home from the (greengrocer, <u>library</u>, factory).

5 As the (elephants, lions, bears) waded across the (high street, river, mountain) they held their (passengers, trunks, suitcases) up high to keep them out of the water.

6 At four o'clock we cross the (lake, road, shop) outside school, looking left and (behind, wrong, right) because of the busy (traffic, police car, day).

7 John quickly (ran, tripped, crept) up the pitch dribbling the (bib, ball, secret) and scored the first (goal, test, baby) of the match.

8 As it is cold outside in the (fridge, playground, classroom), please (put on, take off, eat) your (shoes, coats, apples).

9 Clare, please sharpen your (pen, book, pencil) (over, under, beside) the (bed, mouse, bin).

10 I am already halfway through my very (exciting, eager, delicate) new (pillow, label, book) in the sixth (word, chapter, line).

If $V = 10$, $W = 4$, $X = 3$, $Y = 1$ and $Z = 2$, find the answer to the following calculations.

11 $\frac{V}{Z}$ = _____ 12 $(YZ) + W$ = _____ 13 $(XY) - Z$ = _____ 14 VW = _____

Solve the problems by working out the letter codes. The alphabet has been written out to help you.

A B C D E F G H I J K L M N O P Q R S T U V W X Y Z

Example In a code, SECOND is written as UGEQPF. Decode VJKTF. _THIRD_

15 In a code, WEDGE is written as UCBEC. Decode UCCB. _____

16 In a code, STERN is written as RSDQM. Decode EHQL. _____

17 In a code, HARSH is written as JCTUJ. Decode JWTV. _____

18 In a code, BIRCH is written as CJSDI. Decode GPVS. _____

19 In a code, RIFLE is written as QHEKD. Decode KHED. _____

20 In a code, BADGE is written as CBEHF. Decode CJSE. _____

Total

Test 28: **Mixed**

Underline the two words which are made from the same letters.

Example TAP   PET   <u>TEA</u>   POT   <u>EAT</u>

1	PERCH	CHURCH	PEACH	CHIRP	CHEAP
2	TOAST	STOAT	START	TASTE	ROAST
3	CARTS	SHARK	TRACE	STARK	CRATE
4	PRAISE	ASLEEP	STRIPE	PLEASE	SPITE
5	STRAW	WASPS	STATE	SPATE	TASTE

Choose two words, one from each set of brackets, to complete the sentence in the best way.

Example   Smile is to happiness as (drink, <u>tear</u>, shout) is to (whisper, laugh, <u>sorrow</u>).

6 Pork is to pig as (chops, beef, fish) is to (sheep, cow, chicken).

7 Television is to watch as (radio, ladder, chair) is to (talk, sound, listen).

8 Red is to pink as (black, colour, paint) is to (dark, grey, white).

9 Sunrise is to sunset as (cloudy, afternoon, dawn) is to (dusk, morning, breakfast).

10 Carrot is to vegetable as (cabbage, apple, lettuce) is to (pear, potato, fruit).

11 Kitchen is to cook as (bathroom, bedroom, playroom) is to (sleep, eat, drive).

Some girls were asked which books they had with them in their bags one afternoon.
Ann, Mira and Chloe had spelling books.
Davina and Ann had library books.
Beth had a photo album.
Mira and Chloe had Maths books.
They all had reading books except for Mira.

12 Who had a spelling book as well as a library book? _____

13 Who did not have a Maths or a library book? _____

14 Who had a reading book and a Maths book? _____

15 How many books did Ann have? _____

Solve the problems by working out the codes.

16 If the code for CATCH is LMNLO, what is the code for CHAT? _____

17 If the code for BOOKS is ARRNT, what is the code for SOB? _____

18 If the code for ACTOR is FBYBS, what is the code for ROTA? _____

19 If the code for TRAIN is CZALP, what is the code for ART? _____

20 If the code for PATCH is WZLTO, what is the code for PACT? _____

Total

TEST 29: Mixed

Test time: 0 |||||||||| 5 |||||||||| 10 minutes

Find the letter which will end the first word and start the second word.

Example   peac (h) ome

1   cra (____) oxes   **2**   gir (____) ast   **3**   dog (____) oup   **4**   bat (____) arp

Underline the word in each line that has its letters in alphabetical order.

5	fast	force	fixes	first	fusion
6	abacus	alert	accent	actual	agent
7	blood	blot	blame	blown	bloom
8	hinge	height	hippo	humus	hilly

If the letters of the alphabet are coded as A = 1, B = 2, C = 3 and so on, what words would these codes make?

9   10   1   4   5   _____

10   9   3   5   4   _____

Encode these words using the same code as above.

11   FADE   _____   **12**   HEED   _____

Read the statements and then underline two of the five options below that must be true given the information.

13–14   'Cars and vans are vehicles. All vehicles travel on the road.'
Only vans travel on the road.
Cars travel on roads.
All vehicles are cars.
Vans drive fast.
Roads are for vehicles to travel on.

15–16   'Lions and tigers are related. They are all members of the cat family.'
My cat is a lion.
My cat is related to a lion.
All cats are tigers.
The cat family includes tigers.
Lions eat tigers.

Give the missing numbers in the following sequences.

Example   2   4   6   8   10   _12_

17	3	4	____	9	13	18
18	7	____	15	19	23	27
19	16	18	20	____	24	26
20	20	18	16	14	____	10

(30)

Total [   ]

Find and underline the two words which need to change places for the sentence to make sense.

Example   She went to <u>letter</u> the <u>write</u>.

1   Is the bottom of the garden there at a shed.

2   The road stopped at the bottom of the bus.

3   Jake for eggs and bacon had breakfast.

4   Go please to bed now.

5   The trees fell off the leaves.

6   She in her fork and knife put the dishwasher.

Underline two words, one from each group, that go together to form a new word. The word in the first group always comes first.

Example   (hand, <u>green</u>, for)   (light, <u>house</u>, sure)

7   (quarter, whole, half)   (turn, size, some)

8   (bent, side, up)   (cash, fall, set)

9   (for, in, by)   (spot, deed, date)

10   (wind, black, screw)   (wood, screen, barn)

Here are the number codes for four words. Match the right code to the right word.

MAST	SAME	TEAM	MEET
1446	1836	3814	6481

11   MAST   _____   12   TEAM   _____

13   SAME   _____   14   MEET   _____

Using the same code, decode:

15   3486   _____

Underline the one word which **cannot be made** from the letters of the word in capital letters.

Example   STATIONERY   stone   tyres   ration   <u>nation</u>   noisy

16   BROADEST   strode   trade   breast   toads   dearest

17   BECAUSE   sauce   beast   cease   case   cubes

18   PLANETS   stale   plant   steal   please   staple

19   BEARING   yearn   grain   brine   bring   brain

20   STRANGER   grate   range   stare   great   eager

Total

TEST 31: **Mixed**

Fill in the crosswords so that all the given words are included. You have been given one letter as a clue in each crossword.

1–3

NOTED   PLANK

SENDS   WARTS

LEAVE

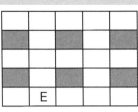

4–6

BRAND   BARBS

DREAD   SHRED

RANGE

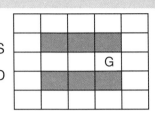

Solve the problems by working out the codes.

7   If 8059 stands for MEND, what is DEN?   _____

8   If % ! $ @ stands for PART, what is TRAP?   _____

9   If BZQU stands for PLAY, what is YAP?   _____

10 If + − = × stands for DOLT, what is TOLD?   _____

Underline the word in the brackets which goes best with the words given outside the brackets.

Example   word, paragraph, sentence   (pen, cap, <u>letter</u>, top, stop)

11   cereal, toast, milk   (curry, marmalade, gravy, wine, beetroot)

12   tail, stripes, fangs   (zebra, wolf, tiger, snail, hippo)

13   sleeve, buttonhole, pocket   (jeans, cloth, scarf, collar, fashion)

Look at these groups of words.

A	**B**	**C**	**D**
elephant	wardrobe	shark	melon
cat	chair	cod	apple
sheep	bed	salmon	peach

Choose the correct group for each of the words below. Write in the letter.

14–16 dogfish ____   cupboard ____   banana ____   table ____   fox ____   grapes ____

Underline the two words, one from each group, which are the most opposite in meaning.

Example   (dawn, <u>early</u>, wake)   (<u>late</u>, stop, sunrise)

17   (spare, whole, eager)   (complete, part, quick)

18   (apart, instant, delicate)   (hardy, course, dainty)

19   (believe, touch, pull)   (find, take, doubt)

20   (open, anxious, free)   (carefree, concerned, careful)

(32)

Total _____

TEST 32: Mixed

Rearrange the letters in capitals to make another word. The new word has something to do with the first two words or phrases.

Example spot soil SAINT __STAIN__

1	jump	hop	PEAL	_____
2	fruit	citrus	MELON	_____
3	silent	peaceful	QUITE	_____
4	snowy	icy rain	STEEL	_____
5	disk	clock face	LAID	_____
6	enchant	dazzle	MARCH	_____

Find a word that can be put in front of each of the following words to make new, compound words.

Example cast fall ward pour __down__

7	card	box	code	man	_____
8	burn	glasses	set	shine	_____
9	hood	proof	like	minder	_____
10	print	path	bridge	ball	_____

If J = 1, K = 2, L = 3, M = 6 and N = 12, find the answer to the following. Write your answer as a letter.

11 J + K + L + M = ____   **12** $\frac{N}{K}$ = ____

13 MK = ____   **14** M − L = ____

Give the missing numbers and letters in the following sequences.

Example 2 4 6 8 10 __12__

15	3	1	____	1	9	1
16	121	222	323	____	525	626
17	18	15	____	9	6	3
18	____	E35	F28	D21	E14	F7
19	96	48	24	12	6	____
20	7	8	10	13	____	22

33

Time for a break! Go to Puzzle Page 45 ▶   Total

Give the missing letters and numbers in the following sequences.
The alphabet has been written out to help you.

A B C D E F G H I J K L M N O P Q R S T U V W X Y Z

Example	CQ	DP	EQ	FP	GQ	HP
1	TH	SH	RI	QI	___	OJ
2	jT	kS	___	mQ	nP	oO
3	E8	F7	G6	___	F4	G3
4	BO	___	FQ	HR	JS	LT
5	___	HJ	IL	JN	KP	LR
6	SF	ME	SD	MC	___	MA

Find the letter which will complete both pairs of words, ending the first word and
starting the second. The same letter must be used for both sets of words.

Example   mea (t) able   fi (t) ub

7	cri (___) ook	sta (___) usy
8	are (___) pple	gal (___) sk
9	dra (___) one	win (___) lory
10	ca (___) oken	goa (___) ail

Find the four-letter word hidden at the end of one word and the beginning of the next
word. The order of the letters may not be changed.

Example   The children had bats and balls.   _sand_

11	Both armies were exhausted.	_____
12	Mary thinks orange juice drinks are best.	_____
13	Pass the netball to Natasha.	_____
14	The head teacher looked quite amused.	_____
15	The bread was stale after a few days.	_____

Underline the two words in each line which are most similar in type or meaning.

Example   <u>dear</u>   pleasant   poor   extravagant   <u>expensive</u>

16	stench	smell	drain	flower	soap
17	join	ear	win	connect	lose
18	push	bend	stretch	curve	shrink
19	compass	rubber	pen	ruler	pencil
20	need	enjoy	bake	dislike	require

(34)

Total

Test 34: **Mixed**

Look at the first group of three words. The word in the middle has been made from the other two words. Complete the second group of three words in the same way, making a new word in the middle.

Example PAIN INTO TOOK ALSO <u>SOON</u> ONLY

1	PAWN	PALE	RULE	WEST	_____	DENT
2	FEEL	FLIP	DRIP	DOOR	_____	CRAB
3	WARN	WADE	TIDE	FACE	_____	CAME
4	SALT	SOME	OMEN	EVEN	_____	ACHE
5	BOTH	KNOT	KNEW	BATH	_____	FLOP

Choose the word or phrase that makes each sentence true.

Example A LIBRARY always has (posters, a carpet, <u>books</u>, DVDs, stairs).

6 A HOTEL always has (restaurants, elevators, bedrooms, air conditioning, a garden).

7 A PEN always has (a lid, a case, ink, a cartridge, a book).

8 A FACE always has (a smile, freckles, glasses, a nose, make up).

9 A RABBIT always has (carrots, a hutch, an owner, long ears, spots).

Here is a plan of a recycling area. From the information below, work out what is recycled in each bin.
Here is a list of the things that are recycled:

River

White Glass

(A)   (B)   (C)   (D)

Cans

(E)   (F)   (G)   (H)

Card is between plastics and shoes and opposite to brown glass.
The glass containers are next to each other by the river.
Green glass is the middle glass container and is not opposite the shoes' bin.

10–15 card _____   shoes _____   plastics _____

green glass _____   brown glass _____   newspapers _____

Find a word that is similar to the word in capital letters and that rhymes with the second word.

Example CABLE tyre <u>wire</u>

16	DRAW	fetch	_____		17	CHICKENS	towel	_____
18	FAST	sick	_____		19	PALE	spite	_____
20	LAW	tool	_____					

35

Total

Fill in the crosswords so that all the given words are included. You have been given one letter as a clue in each crossword.

1–3

SUNNY　PATHS

HONEY　PITCH

TOKEN

4–6

PARCH　KITES

POKER　ROTOR

HOSTS

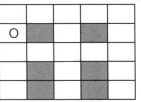

Underline the one word in the brackets which will go equally well with both the pairs of words outside the brackets.

Example　rush, attack　　　cost, fee　　　(price, hasten, strike, <u>charge</u>, money)

7　give, award　　　　　show, exhibit　　　(welcome, card, tell, present, gift)

8　jelly, preserves　　　push, squeeze　　(butter, jam, stick, stuff, pack)

9　intelligent, sharp　　fast, rapid　　　　(swift, prompt, clever, blunt, quick)

10　fine, healthy　　　　hole, water　　　　(fit, drain, pond, well, right)

Remove one letter from the word in capital letters to leave a new word. The meaning of the new word is given in the clue.

Example　AUNT　　an insect　　　　_____ANT_____

11　CLIMB　　　leg　　　　　　　_____

12　BUOY　　　purchase　　　　_____

13　PEARL　　　fruit　　　　　　　_____

14　SPARK　　　public garden　　_____

Fill in the missing letters and numbers. The alphabet has been written out to help you.

A B C D E F G H I J K L M N O P Q R S T U V W X Y Z

Example　AB is to CD as PQ is to <u>RS</u>.

15　TS is to RQ as PO is to ____.

16　Dw is to Ev as Fu is to ____.

17　3XV is to 4WU as 2TR is to ____.

18　FH is to JL as NP is to ____.

19　P11 is to Q9 as R7 is to ____.

20　NL is to JH as MK is to ____.

Total

Give the missing numbers and letters in the following sequences.

Example   5   21   8   17   11   13   <u>14</u>   9

1	S5	R3	S7	R4	S9	R5	___	R6
2	7	12	8	___	9	16	10	18
3	12	11	10	10	8	___	6	8
4	___	z	32	y	24	x	16	w
5	V3	2k	W6	2k	___	2k	Y12	2k

Find the missing number by using the two numbers outside the brackets in the same way as the other sets of numbers.

Example   2 [8] 4   3 [18] 6   5 [25] 5

6	6 [3] 3	5 [1] 4	9 [__] 1
7	12 [4] 3	12 [2] 6	12 [__] 12
8	5 [11] 4	3 [12] 7	5 [__] 3
9	10 [4] 2	6 [1] 3	15 [__] 5

Solve the problems by working out the letter codes. The alphabet has been written out to help you.

A B C D E F G H I J K L M N O P Q R S T U V W X Y Z

Example   In a code, SECOND is written as UGEQPF. Decode VJKTF.   <u>THIRD</u>

10   In a code, SPACE is written as URCEG. Decode ETCD.   _____

11   In a code, STEEP is written as QRCCN. Decode UGJJ.   _____

12   In a code, SLOPE is written as QJMNC. Decode NMJC.   _____

13   In a code, PHONE is written as OGNMD. Decode ONRS.   _____

14   In a code, PLANE is written as RNCPG. Decode NQQR.   _____

15   In a code, DRAIN is written as ESBJO. Decode GJMF.   _____

Underline one word in the brackets which is most opposite in meaning to the word in capitals.

Example   WIDE   (broad   vague   long   <u>narrow</u>   motorway)

16	DEAD	(lifeless	alive	working	gone	arrive)
17	CHEAP	(chick	low	high	expensive	money)
18	HOLD	(twist	hug	release	contain	grip)
19	BRISK	(active	breezy	sluggish	snail	quick)
20	PLAIN	(modest	clear	colour	patterned	frank)

Total

TEST 37: **Mixed**

Test time: 0 ... 5 ... 10 minutes

Here are four number codes: 5793   1375   9375   1379.
Match them to the four words below.

1 DARE _____   **2** BEAR _____

3 READ _____   **4** BEAD _____

Using the same code, decode:

5 19375 _____

Complete the following sentence in the best way by choosing one word from each set of brackets.

Example Tall is to (tree, <u>short</u>, colour) as narrow is to (thin, white, <u>wide</u>).

6 Sheep is to (lamb, wool, hooves) as dog is to (kennel, paws, bark).

7 Bat is to (cricket, tennis, rugby) as stick is to (football, hockey, swimming).

8 Complicated is to (soft, difficult, intelligent) as simple is to (nasty, tricky, easy).

9 Slack is to (hard, loose, strict) as taut is to (rope, tight, tied).

10 Throw is to (catch, fetch, hurl) as cast is to (toss, play, count).

11 Exit is to (hole, entrance, door) as departure is to (arrival, airport, customs).

12–15 Look at these groups of words.

A	B	C	D
India	red	socks	train
England	black	shorts	car
America	green	trousers	bicycle

Choose the correct group for each of the words below. Write in the letter.

Spain _____   shirt _____   yellow _____

orange _____   hat _____   van _____

Norway _____   bus _____

Underline the word in brackets closest in meaning to the word in capitals.

Example UNHAPPY (unkind death laughter <u>sad</u> friendly)

16 RECOVER (bend   send   lend   mend   tend)
17 CARING (mother   kiss   sore   tender   temper)
18 WORTH (bill   time   value   add   money)
19 EMPTY (filled   hollow   heavy   bursting   flooded)
20 UNAWARE (ignorant   aware   beware   mind   awful)

38

Total _____

Test time: 0 | | | | | 5 | | | | 10 minutes

In each line underline the word which would come in the middle if the words were arranged in alphabetical order. The alphabet has been written out to help you.

A B C D E F G H I J K L M N O P Q R S T U V W X Y Z

1	hinge	higher	hello	harder	house
2	stork	stone	story	storm	stool
3	patrol	pattern	pathos	paths	patch
4	frame	fringe	frown	front	frost
5	torch	touch	teach	tooth	train

Underline the one word which **can be made** from the letters of the word in capital letters.

Example CHAMPION camping notch peach cramp <u>chimp</u>

6	FAMOUSLY	mouse	yours	flame	flour	mauls
7	BASKET	token	bathe	skate	tasty	fable
8	ANOTHER	thorny	train	hotter	throne	notes
9	BIRTHDAY	youth	braid	bathe	death	hardly
10	GARDENS	snare	green	snore	drain	sender

Move one letter from the first word and add it to the second word to make two new words.

Example hunt sip _____hut_____ _____snip_____

11	flan	sea	_____	_____
12	year	brain	_____	_____
13	snore	bed	_____	_____
14	heath	torn	_____	_____

Give the missing letters and numbers in the following sequences.
The alphabet has been written out to help you.

A B C D E F G H I J K L M N O P Q R S T U V W X Y Z

Example CQ DP EQ FP GQ <u>HP</u>

15	KL	JL	IM	HM	____	FN
16	Z3	Y5	Z7	Y9	____	Y13
17	____	Hq	Ip	Jo	Kn	Lm
18	FG	IH	____	ML	NO	QP
19	UJ	____	WH	XG	YF	ZE
20	MO	ON	QM	____	UK	WJ

(39)

Total [　　　　　]

Underline the pair of words most similar in meaning.

Example   come, go   <u>roam, wander</u>   fear, fare

1	bizarre, weird	perfect, misshapen	green, grass
2	appreciate, ignore	prize, value	effort, laziness
3	out, in	beside, underneath	near, by
4	precious, valuable	priceless, worthless	costly, cheap
5	rags, riches	tatters, shreds	scraps, cloth

Change the first word into the last word by changing one letter at a time and making a new, different word in the middle.

Example   CASE   _____CASH_____   LASH

6	DOTE	_____	DARE
7	COAT	_____	BEAT
8	CAST	_____	CURT
9	RAIN	_____	PAIR

If A = 12, B = 10, C = 6, D = 5 and E = 2, find the answers to the following calculations. Give the answer to each calculation as a letter.

10 $\frac{A}{C} =$ ____   **11**   (A – B) × D =   ____

12   D × E =   ____   **13**   (C × E) – B =   ____

Read the statements and then underline two of the five options that must be true given the information.

14–15   'The Atlantic is an ocean. Oceans surround the lands of the world.'

There are four oceans in the world.
The Atlantic is one of the world's oceans.
Oceans are large bodies of water.
There are oceans in the world.
Whales live in the Atlantic Ocean.

Solve the problems by working out the codes.

16   If & * \ / stands for WING, & * / stands for _____.

17   If < % ! ? stands for WAIT, < ! ? stands for _____.

18   If + x x ~ stands for PEEK, ~ x x + stands for _____.

19   If $ * / ^ stands for MOAT, / ^ * $ stands for _____.

20   If > ; ; < stands for TOOL, < ; > stands for _____.

(**40**)

Total [   ]

Test time: 0 | | | | | 5 | | | | | 10 minutes

If the letters of the alphabet are coded as A = 1, B = 2, C = 3 and so on, what words would these codes make?

1 8945 _____ **2** 6554 _____

Encode these words using the same code as above.

3 DICE _____
4 CAGED _____
5 DEAF _____

Change one word so that the sentence makes sense. Underline the word you are taking out and write your new word on the line.

Example I waited in line to buy a <u>book</u> to see the film. _____ticket_____

6 Here is a plate to spread the jam on your toast. _____
7 The flash of thunder lit up the night sky. _____
8 The sheepdog guided the flock of seagulls down the hillside. _____
9 As a family we recycle bottles, cans, cardboard and newsagent. _____
10 A policeman helped the old car cross the road and carried his shopping bags for him. _____
11 As the traffic lights turned to red, the cars started to move forwards. _____

Four dogs were judged at a dog show out of a total of twenty marks.

The Beagle scored half marks.
The Alsatian only lost 4 marks out of 20.
The Dalmatian got 5 more marks than the Beagle but 3 less than the Collie.

12 How many marks did the Dalmatian receive? _____
13 Which dog won the competition? _____
14 How many marks did the Beagle receive? _____
15 Which dog did better than the Beagle, but not as well as the Alsatian? _____

Underline the two words which are the odd ones out in the following groups of words.

Example black <u>king</u> purple green <u>house</u>

16	run	pet	crawl	baby	walk
17	quick	rapid	fast	slow	kind
18	remove	blanket	cover	spread	carry
19	cage	frame	coop	crayon	pen
20	friendly	rude	cheerful	scowling	pleasant

41

Total

Puzzle ❶

Help to build a bridge across the crocodile infested river. Use the word boxes at the bottom of the page to make words that link together – the last two letters of the first word make the first two letters of the next word.

The first word has been placed for you.

| LI |
| FE |
| |
| |

AL	SE
ST	NE
RE	UN
TO	IN
EL	OK
TO	SO

Puzzle ❷

Start at the top of the pile of bricks and, working through the layers, make new words by combining two words, one from one layer and the other from the layer below it.

You must go down each time, not sideways.

Here is an example:

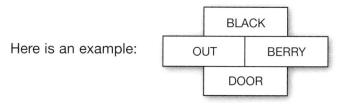

Both BLACKOUT and BLACKBERRY are new words, but only

OUTDOOR makes sense as the next word.

Now try these. Be careful, there is only one path through!

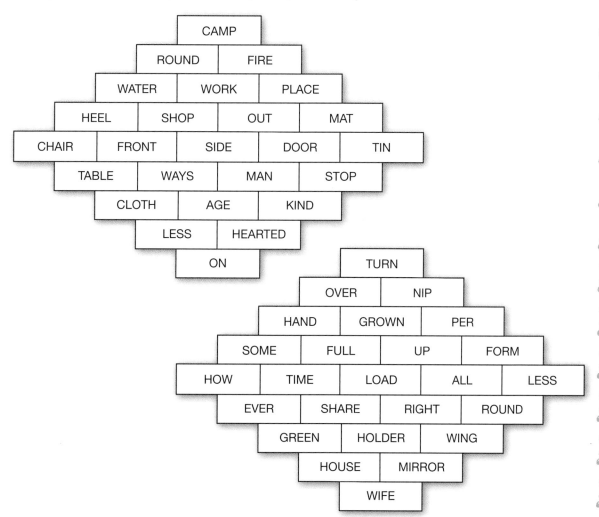

Puzzle ❸

Sarah is tired and wants to go home.

There are several routes that will take her home, but her mother wants her to use a specific one. She has given Sarah written instructions to follow.

Unfortunately, Sarah's older brother has placed three other sets of instructions in Sarah's backpack. Which is the correct set of instructions to take her back home?

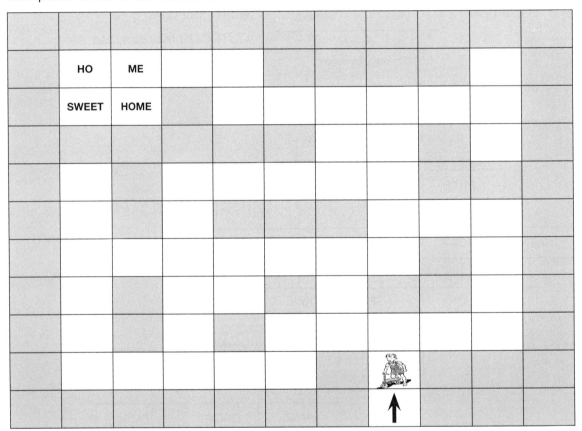

The letters show the compass directions (north, south, east, west). The numbers show the number of squares Sarah should travel (for example, N1 means go north, 1 square).

Here are the four sets of instructions:

A	B	C	D
N1	N1	N1	N1
W1	W2	E2	W1
N2	S1	N3	N2
W3	W4	W2	E1
N2	N3	N3	N4
E4	E2	W3	E2
S2	N2	N1	N1
W4	W1	W2	W1

Puzzle 4

In the centre of each flower is a word. Write a word on each of the petals that can be made using the letters of the centre word. You may only use each letter once. Each word must be three or more letters long.

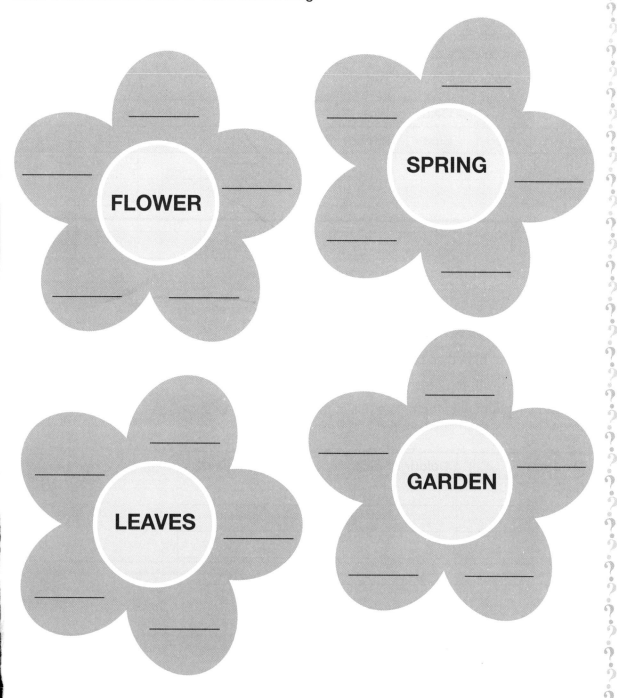

Puzzle 5

Mia, Nathan, Rohan and Sita played a game of dice. Each of them had a pair of different coloured dice – red, blue, yellow or green. The idea of the game was to throw as many sixes as they could in 20 throws. They ended up throwing 5, 7, 12 and 14 sixes.

Using the grid and clues below, work out which colour dice each child had and how many sixes he or she threw.

The first clue has been done for you.

	Colour of dice					Number of sixes			
	Red	**Blue**	**Yellow**	**Green**		**5**	**7**	**12**	**14**
Mia			✗	✗				✔	
Nathan									
Rohan									
Sita									

Clues:

1. Mia scored 12 sixes. Mia does not have yellow or green dice.
2. Nathan has yellow dice.
3. Rohan has blue dice but has not thrown 7 sixes.
4. The child with the green dice has the lowest score.

Your grid should now be complete. Fill in the table below to show the number of sixes each child scored and their dice colour.

Children	Colour of dice	Number of sixes
Mia		
Nathan		
Rohan		
Sita		